Book 1
Excel Shortcuts

BY SAM KEY

&

Book 2
Windows 8 Tips for Beginners

BY SAM KEY

Book 1
Excel Shortcuts

BY SAM KEY

The 100 Top Best Powerful Excel Keyboard Shortcuts in 1 Day!

Table Of Contents

Introduction

I want to thank you and congratulate you for purchasing the book, "The Power of Excel Shortcuts: The 100 Top Best Powerful Excel Keyboard Shortcuts in 1 Day!".

This book contains proven steps and strategies on how to master the Microsoft Excel through just 100 keyboard shortcuts! However, most people will ask, "Why do you need to learn these shortcuts anyway?"

Advantages of Using Microsoft Excel

Microsoft Excel has become one of the most commonly used enterprise software in schools and offices. Its way of presenting data, which is through a spreadsheet, has helped a lot of people especially in the field of data mining. If you were going to put numerous rows of data, in let's say, a word processing program, it might take a lot of time creating tables and formatting each of them to fit in the pages. With the Microsoft Excel, these manual tasks are now much easier.

What does the Microsoft Excel have that other programs don't? For one, it has a built-in spreadsheet that you can manipulate the size and formatting. This versatile way of maneuvering the spreadsheet made it indispensable for many. Now, gone are the days were people have to manually draw tables in sheets of paper. Excel has already the tables prepared for them.

Another nifty feature of this software is its calculation function. Excel houses a myriad of formulas for solving arithmetic, financial and logical problems, among others. Thus, one doesn't even need to calculate every sum or average of a data series. Just by using a formula in Excel, everything can be done in an instant.

The Secret behind Mastering Excel

Speaking of instant, did you know that Excel has more than a hundred keyboard shortcuts? What does this mean to you as an Excel user? It means you can continuously work on your Excel spreadsheet without having to depend on your mouse constantly for Excel functions.

This is especially helpful whenever you are inputting a lot of data, and doing this will be more efficient if both of your hands weren't switching from keyboard to mouse and vice versa, every once in a while. In addition, if your mouse suddenly chose the most inopportune time to malfunction, learning Excel shortcuts can save you from major headaches.

As such, this book will provide you 100 keyboard shortcuts which you can use in Excel. In addition, as a bonus, you will learn about alternatives in case you forget any of these shortcuts.

Thanks again for purchasing this book, I hope you enjoy it!

Chapter 1: Moving Around the Excel Screen

People typically use the mouse for navigating the Excel screen. With this device, you can manipulate every cell in Excel, including its formatting and color. Since the mouse can access the major functions in Excel through the ribbon, there is no need for you to manually-type every formula or command.

However, the only difficult thing that you cannot do with a mouse is entering text. If you're going to use an on-screen keyboard, keying in the data in every cell would probably take you a lot longer than just using the keyboard for the text.

Thus, if you're going to use the keyboard most of the time, especially if you're just starting to build the spreadsheet data from scratch, it would be helpful to learn the basic keyboard shortcuts for moving around the Excel spreadsheet.

Shortcut #1: Arrow Keys

There are four arrow keys found in the right side of your main keyboard keys. These are the Arrow Left, Arrow Right, Arrow Up, and Arrow Down keys. Intuitively, you know that you can use these keys for moving within the spreadsheet. For instance, by selecting a cell then pressing Arrow Up, it will situate the cursor in the cell directly above your selected cell.

Shortcut #2: Ctrl + Arrow Key

Let's assume that you have a block of Excel data that spans more than 50,000 rows and more than 200 columns. You would probably have a hard time using a mouse in skimming these voluminous data. As such, you can use the Ctrl + Arrow key to navigate each "ends" of the data easily. In this example, click any cell in the block of data then press Ctrl + Arrow Down. You will be immediately located to the bottom cell in that specific column.

Shortcut #3: Shift + Arrow Key

You have selected all the items in the row but you forgot to include one cell. What would you do if you needed to include the next cell in the selection? Simply press Shift + Arrow Key, where the arrow pertains to the direction of the region you want to highlight.

Shortcut #4: Ctrl + Shift + Arrow Key

The above shortcut only includes one cell in the selection; but what would happen if you want to include everything until the last cell containing a data? You then use the Ctrl + Shift + Arrow Key.

Shortcut #5: Backspace

The Backspace key immediately deletes the contents of the active cell. However, if the cell is in Edit mode, it will only delete one character in the left of the insertion point, or the blinking cursor in the Formula bar.

Shortcut #6: Delete

This key has the same function as the Backspace key. However, instead of the left side, it removes a character in the right hand side of the insertion point.

Shortcut #7: End

Pressing the End key will enable the End Mode in Excel. In this mode, if you press an Arrow key, it will directly take you to the last used cell (or if none, last cell) in that specific direction. However, if the Scroll Lock is on, pressing the End key will only take you to the lower right corner of your Excel screen.

Shortcut #8: Ctrl + End

It works the same as the End key where pressing this combination will take you to the last used cell. However, if no cells were used, it will not move to the end of the worksheet like the End key does. Also, if the insertion point is located in the Formula bar (e.g., after the first character), Ctrl + End will put this cursor at the end of the field.

Shortcut #9: Ctrl + Shift + End

This keyboard shortcut can do two functions. First, in the Formula bar, it will select every character at the right of the insertion point. On the other hand, if you use it in the worksheet, it will highlight the cells starting from the active cell (or selected cell) until the last used cell in the worksheet.

Shortcut #10: Spacebar

Aside from putting a space in your text, it can also either select or clear a checkbox.

Shortcut #11: Ctrl + Spacebar

This will select the whole column to where the active cell is located.

Shortcut #12: Shift + Spacebar

It has the same function as the above, but this shortcut selects rows instead of columns.

Shortcut #13: Ctrl + Shift + Spacebar

Pressing these keys will select your entire worksheet.

Shortcut #14: Enter

After you have entered a data in a cell, pressing the Enter key will complete the input of data. Besides that, you can also directly go one cell below through this key. Considered as the most commonly used shortcut in Excel, you will be using the Enter key quite a lot because all Excel functions need it.

Shortcut #15: Shift + Enter

If you press Enter, you will go down one cell. Conversely, a Shift + Enter will complete an entry in a cell but the cursor will go directly above your entry.

Shortcut #16: Ctrl + Enter

Since this is a spreadsheet, it follows that after you have put an entry, you will enter another data below it. That is the common task whenever you're working on a table or database, which explains why the Enter key goes down. However, if you think that you need the downward movement, you can try Ctrl + Enter. This will plainly enter your data in the cell and it won't move your cursor to another direction.

Shortcut #17: Alt + Enter

You want the data to go into the next line in the same cell. However, if you press Enter, the cursor just moves on to the next cell in line. Pressing the Tab key doesn't work either. So what will you do? Try Alt + Enter key and see if it works.

Shortcut #18: Esc Key

The Escape key, or simply "Esc", performs a lot of nifty functions in Excel. Among of which are the following: 1) deletes a whole data in a cell, 2) exits you from a dialog box, and 3) escapes you from the full screen mode of Excel.

Shortcut #19: Home Key

The Home key will take you to the first cell in the specific row of your active cell. However, if the Scroll Lock is on, the cursor will go to the upper-left corner of your current window.

Shortcut #20: Ctrl + Home

This shortcut, also known as the "True Home key", brings the user to the beginning of the worksheet.

Shortcut #21: Ctrl + Shift + Home

This will select all cells from the active cell up to the first cell in the worksheet.

Shortcut #22: Page Down

Scouring among rows and rows of worksheets is now easy because of this button. This will display the next page in your Excel window.

Shortcut #23: Alt + Page Down

Unlike Page Down, the Alt + Page Down combination will show the next page to the right of your current window.

Shortcut #24: Ctrl + Page Down

Flipping in several worksheets is now easy thanks to Ctrl + Page Down. This will automatically turn you over to the next worksheet.

Shortcut #25: Ctrl + Shift + Page Down

The normal way of selecting several worksheets at once is to hold Ctrl while clicking each of the worksheets to be included in the selection.

However, for those who don't think this is the practical way to do it, here's an alternative. Use the Ctrl + Shift + Page Down; it will automatically select the sheets for you.

Shortcut #26: Page Up

This is quite similar to Shortcut #22: Page Down key, except for the fact that this one goes in the opposite direction (which is upward).

Shortcut #27: Alt + Page Up

The Alt + Page Up will move your screen to the left, instead of right as what was described in Shortcut #23: Alt + Page Down.

Shortcut #28: Ctrl + Page Up

Same as Shortcut #24: Ctrl + Page Down, this will enable you to change sheets easily. However, this one goes in a counterclockwise direction.

Shortcut #29: Ctrl + Shift + Page Up

Selecting sheets is also a function of the Ctrl + Shift + Page Up. However, it will select the worksheets on the left hand side of your current sheet first.

Shortcut #30: Tab Key

Using the Tab key will enable you to move to the right hand side of the cell. Also, if you have a protected worksheet, pressing this can immediately take you to the next unlocked cell. Lastly, in case there is a dialog box, you can easily move along the options through the Tab key.

Programming Box Set #67: Excel Shortcuts & Windows 8 Tips for Beginners

Shortcut #31: Shift + Tab

The Shift + Tab works the opposite way; if pressing Tab will take you to the right hand cell, this shortcut will locate the left cell for you. It also applies to the other functions of the Tab key. In a dialog box for instance, keying in Shift + Tab will move you to the previous option.

Shortcut #32: Ctrl + Tab

You're now done with shortcuts for moving around cells and worksheets. As such, the succeeding shortcuts in this chapter will focus on dialog boxes. For this shortcut, use it if you want to go to the next tab in a dialog box.

Shortcut #33: Ctrl + Shift + Tab

However, if you wish to go back to the previous tab in a dialog box, using the Ctrl + Shift + Tab is the right combination.

So there you have it, the first 33 keyboard shortcuts in Excel. Hopefully, through these tips you can know traverse in your multitude of cells and worksheets with no difficulty at all.

Chapter 2: Navigating the Excel Ribbon

Microsoft created the "ribbon" as a replacement to the expanding menus in the earlier versions of Microsoft Excel. It houses all the functions in Excel such as formatting, page layout, pictures, and shapes. However, since its interface is not in an expanding menu style, people are not that familiar with its keyboard shortcuts as compared to before where you can immediately see which shortcut runs which.

To help you with that, here are some of the most commonly used keyboard shortcuts for exploring the Ribbon.

Shortcut #34: Alt Key

Letters and numbers will appear in the ribbon once you push the Alt key. What happens is that it activates the access keys, wherein typing in corresponding letter or number will let you select a specific function in the ribbon.

Shortcut #35: F10

This key has the same function as the Alt key, only that pressing the F10 would require you to use your right hand instead.

Shortcut #36: Alt + Arrow Left/Right

To be able to navigate to the other tabs, use these keys.

Shortcut #37: F10 + Arrow Left/Right

Since it was previously mentioned that the F10 behaves the same way as the Alt key, pressing F10 followed by an arrow to the left or to the right will also transfer you to other tabs.

Programming Box Set #67: Excel Shortcuts & Windows 8 Tips for Beginners

Shortcut #38: Ctrl + F1

There's no doubt that the ribbon indeed takes up quite a lot of space in your screen. Therefore, for those who want more area for their spreadsheet, hiding the ribbon is the best option. To do that, simply press Ctrl + F1. To show the ribbon again, also press the same shortcut.

Shortcut #39: Shift + F10

Shift + F10 is similar to the right click button of your mouse. It can open menus and other options depending on where your cursor is.

Shortcut #40: F6

You can move along three areas of the screen through this key. The F6 key, will take you either to the ribbon, the spreadsheet, or the status bar.

Shortcut #41: F10 + Tab

In a tab, you can browse through the functions by pressing this combination continuously. You can also press this shortcut first, and then proceed with the arrow keys for navigation.

Shortcut #42: F10 + Shift + Tab

The above shortcut goes around the functions in a clockwise manner. On the contrary, the F10 + Shift + Tab shortcut does otherwise.

Shortcut #43: F1

In the upper right corner of the ribbon, there is a blue question mark icon. Accessing this icon will take you to the Microsoft Excel Help task pane. Alternatively, if you press F1 the same pane will open.

Since the area around the ribbon is limited, it is only appropriate that there would be less keyboard shortcuts dedicated for it. All in all, there are ten button combinations for the ribbon.

Chapter 3: Formatting the Excel Spreadsheet

If you're also a user of the Microsoft Word, you are probably familiar with formatting keyboard shortcuts such as Ctrl + B, which stands for bold text or Ctrl + I, which italicizes your text. Since you can do almost every basic feature that you need in the Word application through the keyboard, this makes the formatting easier for you.

Fortunately, even though Excel is not a word-processing program, it also has dedicated keyboard shortcuts that for formatting. These are as follows:

Shortcut #44: Alt + '

By going to the Styles group in the Home tab, you can quickly change the appearance of the cell by selecting any of the pre-installed styles in Excel. To see the formatting changes done within a cell, you click on the New Style option, which will take you to the Style dialog box. Similarly, clicking Alt + ' will get you in the same menu.

Shortcut #45: Ctrl + B

Like in Microsoft Word, Ctrl + B will either apply or remove a bold format in a text.

Shortcut #46: Ctrl + 2

This shortcut can also make the selected text into a bold type.

Shortcut #47: Ctrl + I

Letter I stands for Italics. As such, clicking Ctrl + I will turn any text into an italicized type.

Shortcut #48: Ctrl + 3

This also functions like the Ctrl + I shortcut.

Shortcut #49: Ctrl + U

Ctrl + U will put an underline in the selected text.

Shortcut #50: Ctrl + 4

Another alternative for the Ctrl +U is the Ctrl + 4 shortcut.

Shortcut #51: Ctrl + 5

To easily put a strikethrough in your text, press Ctrl + 5.

Shortcut #52: Ctrl + Shift + F

If you want more font formatting options, you can just proceed to the Font tab of the Format cells dialog box. Right-clicking a cell then selecting Format Cells will get you there, or you can just use this shortcut.

Shortcut #53: Ctrl + Shift + P

This shortcut works the same as the above.

Shortcut #54: Ctrl + Shift + &

Now that you're done with editing the text, this shortcut as well as the succeeding ones will pertain to cell formatting. As for Ctrl + Shift + &, it will put a plain black border on all sides of the cell.

Shortcut #55: Ctrl + Shift + _

On the contrary, Ctrl + Shift + _ will remove the borders that you have made.

Shortcut #56: F4

Instead of manually doing all the formatting for a number of cells, Excel has a shortcut wherein you can redo the formatting that you just did in another cell. This is the F4 function key. For example, if you have put borders in Cell A1, selecting Cell A2 then pressing F4 will also create borders for that specific cell.

Shortcut #57: Ctrl + 1

Pressing the Ctrl + 1 will show the Format Cells dialog box. In this box, you can edit every possible formatting for a cell such as number format, alignment, font, border, and fill.

The previous chapters have discussed how certain shortcuts can perform specific functions in Excel such as formatting cells and navigating the spreadsheet. In the following chapters, the topics will be about the different uses of specific buttons such as the Function keys and the Control key.

Chapter 4: Working with Function Keys

The first row of keys in your keyboard contains the function keys, which is denoted by the letter F followed by a number. In the Windows desktop, these function keys can do a variety of tasks such as adjusting the screen brightness or minimizing the volume.

Excel uses the function keys for different purposes. Thus, most people usually have a difficulty mastering the Function key shortcuts in Excel.

Shortcut #58: Alt + F1

Alt + F1 will automatically create a chart for you. Just select the range of cells containing your chart data then press this shortcut. Afterwards, a column chart will appear in the worksheet.

Shortcut #59: Alt + Shift + F1

The normal way in creating a new worksheet is by right-clicking any of the existing worksheets then choosing Insert. The same task can be done by this shortcut.

Shortcut #60: F2

In editing a formula, you can't just simply select an active cell; you have to click on the Formula bar so that you can make changes to it. Fortunately, the F2 will put the cell in Edit mode. Thus, if you want to amend a cell, there's no need for you to click on the Formula bar; just use F2 instead.

Shortcut #61: Shift + F2

The Shift + F2 shortcut will insert comments in the active cell.

Shortcut #62: Ctrl + F2

Unlike the previous F2 combinations, this one has nothing to do with editing a cell. When you press Ctrl + F2, you will be forwarded to the Print Preview screen. Upon exiting this screen, your spreadsheet will show dotted lines which serves as a marker for a page border.

Shortcut #63: F3

Instead of constantly referring to a range of cells by their cell location (e.g., A1:D1), you can just define a name for this range. Thus, whenever you want to pertain to that specific range in a formula, you can simply put its name; there's no need for you to put the cell range. F3 will take you to the Paste Name dialog box, wherein you can list all the names created in a worksheet and their respective cell references.

Shortcut #64: Ctrl + F3

To create a new name, go to the Name Manager through Ctrl + F3.

Shortcut #65: Shift + F3

Using formulas is the heart of Microsoft Excel. Without it, you cannot do any calculations in the spreadsheet. As such, there is a dedicated tab for Formulas in the Excel ribbon. However, it may take quite a lot of time for users to efficiently look for the appropriate formula with all the possible options in the Formulas tab. Because of this, the Shift + F3 key combination is made. It opens the Insert Function dialog box, wherein you can easily search for a formula by just typing in the description of what you need to do.

Shortcut #66: Ctrl + F4

You don't need to click that "X" mark in the upper left corner of your Excel screen just to close the application; a simple Ctrl + F4 is enough to do the job.

Shortcut #67: F5

Rummaging through a lot of cells takes a lot of work, especially if you're dealing with thousands of rows in a spreadsheet. The Go To dialog box, which can be accessed through F5, will help you reach that specific cell or range that you wanted to see.

Shortcut #68: Ctrl + F5

By default, all workbooks are always in full screen mode in Excel. However, if you're doing work on several Excel files at once, it may be hard to switch from one file to the other when each workbook is on full screen. Through Ctrl + F5, the selected file restore to window size in the Excel screen so that you can easily switch across files.

Shortcut #69: Shift + F6

This works the same as Shortcut #40: F6, albeit in a counterclockwise direction.

Shortcut #70: Ctrl + F6

If you have more than one workbook open, pressing Ctrl + F6 will let you switch among these workbooks.

Shortcut #71: F7

Aside from Microsoft Word, the Excel application has also a built-in spell checker. To check the spelling of every word in your spreadsheet, press F7. This will run the Spelling dialog box. Apart from detecting erroneous spellings, it also suggests possible words that can replace the incorrect word.

Shortcut #72: Ctrl + F7

As mentioned before, you should not use the full screen mode when working with several Excel files. This is so that you can select each workbook with ease. The Ctrl + F7 shortcut executes the Move command so that you can drag the unneeded workbooks in another area in the Excel screen where it can't obstruct your view.

Shortcut #73: F8

Upon pressing F8, the Excel goes into an Extend Selection mode. This enables you to use the arrow keys to extend the current selection. Pressing the same key will also lift the Extend Selection mode.

Shortcut #74: Shift + F8

The limitation of the F8 key is that it only adds adjacent cells in the selection. Through Shift + F8, you can now add any nonadjacent cell by using arrow keys.

Shortcut #75: Ctrl + F8

To resize your workbook, use Ctrl + F8. This will run the Size command for workbooks that are not in a full screen mode.

Shortcut #76: Alt + F8

A macro is a set of actions created using the Visual Basic programming language. What it does is to automate a set of tasks in Excel. For example, you're going to retrieve a data in a one sheet then you'll paste the said data in another sheet. However, if you're going to do the copy-paste task for thousands of data, it might take you a long time. As such, you can use the macro for this. Alt + F8 will open the Macro dialog box, where you can record and run a macro.

Shortcut #77: F9

This is the Refresh button in Excel. Once you refresh a workbook, it will recalculate all new formulas in the said file.

Shortcut #78: Shift + F9

On the other hand, Shift + F9 will only recalculate the formulas in the worksheet you are currently working on.

Shortcut #79: Ctrl + Alt + F9

This has the same function as F9, but it will also recalculate formulas that have not been changed.

Shortcut #80: Ctrl + Alt + Shift + F9

Aside from doing what the Ctrl + Alt + F9 shortcut does, it also rechecks all dependent formulas for any errors.

Shortcut #81: Alt + Shift + F10

Smart tags are data that are labeled in a particular type. For instance, a person's name in an Outlook email message can be labeled with this tag. You can open the smart tag menu through this shortcut.

Shortcut #82: Ctrl + F10

This will enable a workbook to display in full screen mode (or maximized mode).

Shortcut #83: F11

The Shortcut #58: Alt + F1 will let you create charts by highlighting the data series. Similarly, the F11 key has the same function except that you don't need to select the data series; it will automatically detect the data for you. Another difference between these two shortcuts is that the Alt + F1 will display the chart in the same worksheet, while the F1 key will make another worksheet for the new chart.

Shortcut #84: Shift + F11

This is an alternative to Shortcut #59: Alt + Shift + F1, wherein it will insert a new worksheet.

Shortcut #85: Alt + F11

Alt + F11 will open the Microsoft Visual Basic Editor. In this menu, you can create or edit a macro by using the Visual Basic for Applications (VBA) programming language.

Shortcut #86: F12

The F12 key is the shortcut for the Save As dialog box. It lets you save your Excel file among the available formats.

In case you're wondering why the F1, F4, F6 and F10 keys as well as some of their derivatives are not included in the list, these function keys have already been discussed in the previous chapters. Moreover, as this book specifically claims that it will contain at least a hundred keyboard shortcuts, putting these function keys again in the list will not create an accurate count of all the shortcuts.

Chapter 5: Discovering Ctrl Combinations

There are more than 50 Ctrl key combinations that you can use in the Excel sheet, with some shortcuts comprising of special characters instead of the usual alphanumeric ones. Thus, it would be unpractical to include every possible shortcut, especially if there's a little chance that a typical user will use them all.

With these reasons, only the f14 most valuable Ctrl shortcuts will be contained in the list below.

Shortcut #87: Ctrl + ;

Ctrl + ; will show the current date in the active cell.

Shortcut #88: Ctrl + Shift + #

Ctrl + Shift + # will change the date into a day-month-year format.

Shortcut #89: Ctrl + A

This is an alternative to Shortcut #13: Ctrl + Shift + Spacebar. Pressing these keys will also select the whole worksheet.

Shortcut #90: Ctrl + C

Ctrl + C will copy the contents of the active cell.

Shortcut #91: Ctrl + F

If you need to search for a specific data, you don't have to go to the Home tab and choose Find & Select. By pressing Ctrl + F, you can now access the Find and Replace dialog box immediately.

Programming Box Set #67: Excel Shortcuts & Windows 8 Tips for Beginners

Shortcut #92: Ctrl + K

To insert or edit a hyperlink, use this shortcut.

Shortcut #93: Ctrl + R

This activates the Fill Right command. To use this, simply click on a cell you want filled then press Ctrl + R. It will copy all the formatting and contents of the cell to its left.

Shortcut #94: Ctrl + S

Ctrl + S will automatically save your file in its current name, location and format.

Shortcut #95: Ctrl + V

After doing Shortcut #90: Ctrl + C, you then proceed with Ctrl + V to paste the contents that you have copied.

Shortcut #96: Ctrl + Alt + V

Since the above shortcut will paste all the data as is, the Ctrl + Alt + V will give you most pasting options as it will open the Paste Special dialog box.

Shortcut #97: Ctrl + W

This combination is an alternative to Shortcut #66: Ctrl + F4, which closes the Excel program.

Shortcut #98: Ctrl + X

This will cut the contents of an active cell. When you say "cut", it will remove the data in a cell and will place it temporarily in the Clipboard so that you can paste the contents in another cell.

Shortcut #99: Ctrl + Y

The Ctrl + Y shortcut runs the Redo function, which means that it will repeat the previous command that you have done.

Shortcut #100: Ctrl + Z

Lastly, Ctrl + Z serve as the shortcut for the Undo function. This will reverse your latest command in Excel.

And that finishes our countdown for the Top 100 keyboard shortcuts in Microsoft Excel. To wrap things up, the last chapter will provide some pointers in "memorizing" these shortcuts the easiest way.

Chapter 6: Pointers for the Excel Novice

Most people will most likely feel daunted with the mere volume of shortcuts in this book. "How can I ever memorize a hundred of these combinations?", says most people. This fear of memorization only impedes the learning process. As such, you should stay away from this negative thinking.

Practice a Couple of Shortcuts Every Week

To be able to remember these shortcuts effectively, you should use them as often as you could. Have this book by your side always so that you will have a guide as you try to absorb each of these shortcuts. Better yet, you can jot down a couple of shortcuts in a small list so that you can try some of these tricks in your school or the office.

After finishing let's say at least five shortcuts for a week, add another five in the succeeding weeks. Just don't forget the previous shortcuts that you have learned. In no time, you will be able to use these keyboard combinations without the help of a cheat sheet.

Don't Use the Numeric Keypad

Although most people on the go use laptops such as students, many people still use the full-sized keyboard that has a built-in numeric keypad at the right side.

Although several characters in the listed shortcuts are there, the Microsoft Excel does not recognize the use of numeric keypad in its shortcuts. As such, you shouldn't try to practice these shortcuts via the numeric keypad; just use the main keyboard itself.

That ends all the pointers in this guide for Excel shortcuts. With that, you should apply all the learnings that you have discovered through this book in your daily Excel tasks. Hopefully, you'll be a more efficient Excel user as you incorporate these shortcuts in using the said spreadsheet program.

Conclusion

Thank you again for purchasing this book!

I hope this book was able to help you to learn the secrets behind mastering Microsoft Excel, which are the 100 keyboard shortcuts.

The next step is to make use of these shortcuts every time you operate on the Excel application. Through this, you can now easily work on your Excel spreadsheets with only a minimal use of a mouse.

Finally, if you enjoyed this book, please take the time to share your thoughts and post a review on Amazon. We do our best to reach out to readers and provide the best value we can. Your positive review will help us achieve that. It'd be greatly appreciated!

Thank you and good luck!

Book 2
Windows 8 Tips for Beginners
BY SAM KEY

A Simple, Easy, and Efficient Guide to a Complex System of Windows 8!

Table Of Contents

Introduction

I want to thank you and congratulate you for purchasing the book, "Windows 8 Tips for Beginners: A Simple, easy, and efficient guide to a complex system of windows 8!"

This book contains proven steps and strategies on how to familiarize yourself with the new features of Windows 8 which were designed to make your computing experience simpler and more enjoyable. You will not only learn how to navigate through Windows 8 , but you will also learn how Windows 8 is similar to and different from the older versions so you can easily adjust and take advantage of the benefits that Windows 8 has in store for you.

Thanks again for purchasing this book, I hope you enjoy it!

Chapter 1: How is Windows 8 Different from Previous Versions?

With Windows 8, Microsoft launched a lot of new changes and features, some of which are minor , but others are major. Some of the changes you can see in Windows 8 are the redesigned interface, enhanced security and other online features.

Changes in the Interface

The most glaring change you will observe when you first open your computer with Windows 8 is that the screen looks completely different from older Windows versions. The Windows 8 interface has new features such as Start screen, hot corners, and live tiles.

• The Start screen will be the main screen where you will find all of your installed programs and they will be in the form of "tiles". You can personalize your Start Screen by rearranging the tiles, selecting a background image and changing the color scheme.

• You can navigate through Windows 8 using the "hot corners", which you activate by hovering the mouse pointer over the corners of the screen. For instance, if you want to switch to another open application, hover your mouse in the top-left corner of your screen and then click on the app.

• Certain apps have Live Tile functions, which enable you to see information even if the app itself is not open. For instance, you can easily see the current weather on the Weather app tile from your Start screen; if you want to see more information, you can just click on the app to open it.

• You can now find many of the settings of your computer in the Charms bar that you can open by hovering the mouse in the bottom-right or top-right corner of your computer screen.

Online Features in Windows 8

Programming Box Set #67: Excel Shortcuts & Windows 8 Tips for Beginners

Because of the ease of accessing Internet now, many people have started to save their documents and other data online. Microsoft has made it easier to save on the cloud through their OneDrive service (this was formerly called SkyDrive). Windows 8 is capable of linking to OneDrive and other online social networks such as Twitter and Facebook in a seamless manner.

To connect your computer to OneDrive, sign in using your free Microsoft account instead of your own computer account. When you do this, all of the contacts, files and other information stored in your OneDrive are all in your Start screen. You can also use another computer to sign in to your Microsoft account and access all of your OneDrive files. You can also easily link your Flickr, Twitter and Facebook accounts to Windows 8 so you will be able to see the updates straight from your Start screen. You can also do this through the People app which is included in Windows 8.

Other Features

•   The Desktop is now simpler for enhanced speed. Yes, the Desktop is still included in Windows 8 and you can still manage your documents or open your installed programs through the Desktop. However, with Windows 8, a number of the transparency effects that frequently caused Windows Vista and Windows 7 to slow down are now gone. This allows the Desktop to operate smoother on nearly all computers.

•   The Start menu, once considered as a vital feature in previous Windows versions, is now the Start screen. You can now open your installed programs or search for your files through the Start screen. This can be quite disorienting if you are just starting with Windows 8.

•   Windows 8 has enhanced security because of its integrated antivirus program referred to as Windows Defender. This antivirus program is also useful in protecting you from different kinds of malware. In addition, it can aid in keeping you and your computer secure by telling you which data each of your installed apps can access. For instance, certain apps can access your location, so if you do not want other people to know where you are, just change your preference in the settings/configuration part of your apps.

How to Use Windows 8

Because Windows 8 is not like the older versions, it will possibly change how you have been using your computer. You may need quite some time to get accustomed to the new features, but you just need to remember that those changes are necessary to enhance your computing experience. For instance, if you have used older Windows versions, you may be used to clicking on the Start button to launch programs. You need to get used to using the Start screen with Windows 8. Of course, you can still use the Desktop view to make file and folder organization easier and to launch older programs.

You may need to switch between the Desktop view and the Start screen to work on your computer. Don't feel bad if you feel disoriented at first because you will get used to it. Moreover, if you just use your computer to surf the internet, you may be spending majority of your time in the Start screen anyway.

Chapter 2: How to Get Started with Windows 8

Windows 8 can truly be bewildering at the start because of the many changes done to the interface. You will need to learn effective navigation of both the Start screen and Desktop view. Even though the Desktop view appears similar to the older Windows versions, it has one major change that you need to get used to – the Start menu is no more.

In this chapter, you will learn how to work with the apps and effectively navigate Windows 8 using the Charms bar. You will learn where to look for the features that you could previously find in the Start menu.

How to Sign In

While setting up Windows 8, you will be required to create your own account name and password that you will use to sign in. You can also opt to create other account names and associate each account name with a specific Microsoft account. You will then see your own user account name and photo (if you have uploaded one). Key in your password and press enter. To select another user, click on the back arrow to choose from the available options. After you have signed in, the Start screen will be displayed.

How to Navigate Windows 8

You can use the following ways to navigate your way through Windows 8

•   You can use the hot corners to navigate through Windows 8. You can use them whether you are in the Desktop view or in the Start screen. Simply hover your mouse in the corner of the screen to access the hot corners. You will see a tile or a toolbar that you can then click to open. All the corners perform various tasks. For instance, hovering the pointer on the lower-left corner will return you to the Start screen. The upper-left corner will allow you to switch to the last application that you were using. The lower-right or upper-right corners gives you access to the Charms bar where you can either manage your printers or adjust the settings of your computer. Hover your mouse towards the upper-left corner and then move your mouse down to see the list of the different applications that you are simultaneously using. You can simply on any application to go back to it.

• You can also navigate through Windows 8 through different keyboard shortcuts.

o Alt+Tab is the most useful shortcut; you use it to switch between open applications in both the Start screen and Desktop view.

o You can use the Windows key to go back to the Start screen. It also works in both the Desktop view and Start screen.

o From the Start screen, you can go to the Desktop view by clicking on Windows+D.

• You can access the settings and other features of your computer through the toolbar referred to as Charms bar. Place your mouse pointer on the bottom-right or top-right corner of your screen to display the Charms bar wherein you can see the following icons or "charms":

o The Search charm allows you to look for files, apps or settings on your computer. However, a simpler method to do a search is through the Start screen wherein you can simply key in the name of the application or file that you want to find.

o You can think of the Share charm as a "copy and paste" attribute that is included in Windows 8 to make it easier for you to work with your computer. Using the Share charm, you can "copy" data like a web address or a picture from one app and then "paste" it onto another application. For instance, if you are reading a certain article in the Internet, you can share the website address in your Mail application so you can send it to a friend.

o The Start charm will allow you to go back to the Start screen. If you are currently on the Start screen, the Start charm will launch the latest app that you used.

o The Devices charm displays all of the hardware devices that are linked to your computer such as monitors and printers.

o Through the Settings charm, you can open both the general setting of your computer and the settings of the application that you are presently using. For instance, if you are presently using the web browser, you can access the Internet Options through the Settings charm.

How to Work with the Start Screen Applications

You may need to familiarize yourself with the Start screen applications because they are quite different from the "classic" Windows applications from previous versions. The apps in Windows 8 fill the whole screen rather than launching in a window. However, you can still do multi-tasking by launching two or more applications next to each other.

• To open an application from the Start screen, look for the app that you want to launch and click on it.

• To close an application hover your mouse at the top portion of the application, and you will notice that the cursor will become a hand icon, click and hold your mouse and then drag it towards the bottommost part of the screen and then release. When the app has closed, you will go back to the Start screen.

How to View Apps Side by Side

Even though the applications normally fill up the whole screen, Windows 8 still allows you to snap an application to the right or left side and then launch other applications beside it. For instance, you can work on a word document while viewing the calendar app. Here are the steps to view applications side by side:

1. Go to the Start screen and then click on the first app that you want to open.

2. Once the app is open, click on the title bar and drag the window to the left or right side of your computer screen.

3.   Release your mouse and you will see that the application has snapped to the side of your computer screen.

4.   You can go back to the Start screen by clicking at any empty space of the computer screen.

5.   Click on another application that you want to open.

6.   You will now see the applications displayed side by side. You can also adjust the size of the applications by dragging the bar.

Please note that the snapping feature is intended to work with a widescreen monitor. Your minimum screen resolution should be 1366 x 768 pixels to enjoy the snapping feature fully. If your monitor has a bigger screen, you will be able to snap more than two apps simultaneously.

How to cope with the Start menu

Many people have already complained about the missing Start menu in Windows 8. For many Windows users, the Start menu is a very vital feature because they use to open applications, look for files, launch the Control Panel and shut down their computer. You can actually do all of these things in Windows 8 too, but you will now have to look for them in different locations.

•   There are a number of ways to launch an application in Windows 8. You can launch an app by clicking the application icon on the taskbar or double-clicking the application shortcut form the Desktop view or clicking the application tile in the Start screen.

•   You can look for an app or a file by pressing the Windows key to go back to the Start screen. When you are there, you can simply key in the filename or app name that you want to look for. The results of your search will be immediately displayed underneath the search bar. You will also see a list of recommended web searches underneath the search results.

•   You can launch the Control Panel by going to the Desktop view and then hovering your mouse in the lower-right corner of the computer screen to display the Charms bar and then selecting Settings. From the Settings Pane, look for and choose Control Panel.

After the Control Panel pops up, you can start choosing your preferred settings.

• You can shut down your computer by hovering the mouse in the lower-right corner of your screen to display the Charms bar and then selecting Settings. Click on the Power icon and then choose Shut Down.

Start Screen Options

If you prefer to continue working with the Desktop view more often, you actually have a number of alternatives that can let your computer operate more like the older Windows versions. One of these alternatives is the "boot your computer directly to the Desktop" rather than the Start screen. Here are the steps to change your Start screen options:

1. Return to the Desktop view.

2. Right-click the taskbar then choose Properties.

3. You will then see a dialog box where you can choose the options that you want to change.

Chapter 3: How to Personalize Your Start Screen

If you are open to the idea of spending most of your time on the Start screen of your computer, there are different ways you can do to personalize it based on your preferences. You can change the background color and image, rearrange the applications, pin applications and create application groups.

•   You can change the background of your Start screen by hovering the mouse in the lower-right corner of your screen to open up the Charms bar and then selecting the Settings icon. Choose Personalize and then choose your preferred color scheme and background image.

•   You can change the lock screen picture by displaying the Charms bar again and the selecting the Settings icon. Choose Change PC settings and then choose Lock screen that is located near to the topmost part of the screen. Choose your preferred image from the thumbnail photos shown. You can also opt to click on Browse to choose your own photos. You will see the lock screen every time you return to your computer after leaving it inactive for a set number of minutes. However, you can also manually lock your screen by clicking on your account name and then choosing Lock.

•   You can change your own account photo by displaying the Charms bar and then choosing the Settings icon. Click on the Change PC setting and choose Account picture. You can look for your own photos by clicking Browse, will let you browse the folders in your computer. Once you find the picture you want to use, click on Choose image to set it as your account picture. If you are running a laptop, you can also use the built-in webcam to take a picture of yourself for your account photo.

How to Customize the Start Screen Applications

You do not really need to put up with the pre-arranged apps on your Start screen. You can change how they look by rearranging them based on your own preference. You can move an app by clicking, holding and dragging the application to your preferred location. Let go of your mouse and the app tile will automatically move to the new place.

You may also think that the animation in the live tiles is very disturbing while you are working. Do not worry because you can simply turn the animation off so that you will only see a plain background. You can do this by right-clicking the application that you wish to change. A toolbar pop up from the bottom part of your computer screen. Simply choose Turn live tile off and the animation if you don't want real-time notifications.

How to Pin Applications to the Start Screen

By default, you won't be able to see all of the installed applications on the Start screen. However, you can easily "pin" your favorite apps on the Start screen so you can access them easily. You can do this by clicking the arrow found in the bottom-left corner of your Start screen. You will then see the list of all the applications that you have installed. Look for the app you want to pin and the right-click it. You will see Pin to Start at the lowest part of the screen. Click on it to pin your app.

To unpin or remove an application from the Start screen, right-click the app icon you want to remove and then choose "Unpin from Start".

How to Create Application Groups

There are more ways to bring organization to your apps. One way is to create an app group wherein you can similar apps together. You can give a specific name for each app group for easier retrieval. You can create a new application group by clicking, holding and dragging an application to the right side until you see it on an empty space of the Start screen. Let go of your mouse to let the app be inside its own application group. You will be able to see a distinct space between the new app group that you have just created and the other app groups. You can then drag other apps into the new group.

Programming Box Set #67: Excel Shortcuts & Windows 8 Tips for Beginners

You can name your new application group by right clicking any of the apps on the Start screen and then clicking Name group at the top of the application group. When choosing a group name, opt for shorter, but more descriptive names. After you have keyed in your group name, press the Enter key.

Chapter 4: How to Manage Your Files and Folders

The File Explorer found in the Desktop view is very handy in managing files and folders in your computer. If you are familiar with older Windows version, File Explorer is actually the same as Windows Explorer. You will usually use the File Explorer for opening, accessing and rearranging folders and files in the Desktop view. You can launch the File Explorer by clicking the folder icon found on the taskbar.

The View tab in the File Explorer enables you to alter how the files appear inside the folders. For instance, you may choose to the List view when viewing documents and the Large Icons view when looking at photos. You can change the content view by selecting the View tab and then choosing your preferred view from the Layout group.

For certain folders, you can also sort your files in different ways – by name, size, file type, date modified, date created, among others. You can sort your files by selecting the View tab, clicking on the Sort by button and then choosing your preferred view from the drop-down list.

How to Search Using the File Explorer

Aside from using the Charms bar to look for files, you can also use the Search bar in the File Explorer. Actually, the File Explorer provides search options that are more advanced than those offered by the Charms bar. This is very useful when you are finding it quite hard to look for a particular document.

Every time you key in a word into the search bar, you will see that the Search Tools tab automatically opens on the Ribbon. You can find the advanced search options on the Search Tools tab. You can use them to filter your search by size, file type or date modified. You can also see the latest searches that you have made.

How to Work with Libraries

Windows 8 has 4 main libraries: Documents, Music, Pictures and Videos. Whenever you need a specific file, you can search for them through the Libraries or groups of content that you can readily access via the File Explorer.

The folders and files that you create are not actually stored in the Libraries themselves. The libraries are just there to help you better organize your stuff. You can place your own folders inside the libraries without the need to change their actual location in your computer. For instance, you can place a folder your recent photos in the Pictures library and still keep the folder on your Desktop for ready access.

Libraries are particularly vital in Windows 8 since a lot of the applications on the Start screen such as Photos, Music and Vides use the libraries in looking for and displaying their content. For instance, all of the photos in your Pictures library are also in your Photos app.

You need to note that the applications on your Start screen are optimized for media so that it will be more trouble-free for you to watch videos, listen to music and view your pictures. The File Explorer is an essential tool in organizing your current media files into libraries so that you can easily enjoy them right from your Start screen.

The My Music, My Documents folders and other certain folders are automatically included in their own applicable libraries. But you can add your own folders to any of the Libraries by first locating the Folder you want to add and then right-clicking on it. Choose the Include in library and then choose your preferred library. This technique allows your folder to be both in your library and in its original location.

Chapter 5: How to Get Started with the Desktop

The Start screen really is a cool new feature of Windows 8. But if you will be doing more than surfing the internet, watching videos and listening to music, you need to familiarize yourself with the different features in the Desktop view.

How to Work with Files

The details of the File Explorer were already discussed in the previous chapter. In this chapter, you will learn how to open and delete files, navigate through the various folders, and more.

After you have opened the File Explorer and you instantly see the document that you wish to open, you can simply double-click on it to open it. But if you still need to go through the different folders, the Navigation pane is very useful in choosing a different folder or location.

How to Delete Files

You can delete a file by clicking, holding and dragging the file directly to the Recycle Bin icon found on the Desktop. An easier way is choosing the file that you want to delete and then pressing the Delete key. Do not worry if you have unintentionally deleted a file. You can access the Recycle Bin to locate the deleted file and restore it to its original folder. You can do this by right-clicking the file that you want to restore and then choosing Restore.

But if you are certain that all files in the Recycle Bin can be permanently deleted, you can clear it by right-clicking the Recycle Bin icon and then choosing Empty Recycle bin.

How to Open an Application on the Desktop

You can do this by either clicking the application icon found on the taskbar or double-clicking the application shortcut found on the Desktop.

How to Pin Applications to the Taskbar

By default, only selected application icons will be included on your taskbar. But you can pin your most used application on the taskbar so you can readily access them. You can do this by right-clicking anyplace on the Start screen. You will then see a menu at the bottom of your screen. Choose the All apps button to show the list of all your installed applications. Look for the application you want to pin and the right-click it and then choose Pin to taskbar. You need to note, though, that you cannot pin all applications to your taskbar. There are certain applications that are designed to be launched from the Start screen only like Calendar and Messaging. Thus, you can only pin them to the Start screen.

How to Use Desktop Effects

Multi-tasking and working with several windows have become easier with Windows 8 because of the various Desktop effects now available to you.

• You can use the Snap effect to quickly resize open windows. This is particularly useful when you are working with several windows simultaneously. You can use the Snap effect by clicking, holding and dragging a window to the right or the left until you see the cursor reach the edge of your screen. Release your mouse to snap the window into place. You can easily unsnap a window by clicking, dragging it down and then releasing your mouse.

• Use the Peek effect for viewing the open windows from your taskbar. You can do this by hovering your mouse over any app icon on the taskbar that you want to view. You will then see a thumbnail preview of all open windows. You can view the full-sized window of the application by hovering the mouse over the app in the thumbnail preview.

Programming Box Set #67: Excel Shortcuts & Windows 8 Tips for Beginners

•   Use the Shake feature for selecting a single window from a clutter of open windows and then minimizing the rest. You can do this by locating and selecting the window that you want to concentrate on. You can then gently shake the window back and forth to minimize the other open windows. When you shake the window once more, all of the windows that you minimized will get maximized again.

•   The Flip feature is useful in scrolling across a preview of all your open windows. You can also view any of the open applications on your Start screen using the Flip preview. The first three features – Snap, Shake and Peek – are for use only on the Desktop view. The Flip feature, on the other hand, can be used similarly in both the Desktop view and the Start screen. You can access the Flip preview by pressing and holding the Alt key and then pressing the Tab key. While you are still pressing the Alt key, press the Tab key to continue scrolling through your open windows. When you have spotted the application or the window that you want to view, stop pressing the Alt and Tab keys to display the app or window.

Conclusion

Thank you again for purchasing this book!

I hope this book was able to help you to use the new features of Windows 8.

The next step is to start personalizing your own Windows 8 so you can get the most out of it.

Finally, if you enjoyed this book, please take the time to share your thoughts and post a review on Amazon. We do our best to reach out to readers and provide the best value we can. Your positive review will help us achieve that. It'd be greatly appreciated!

Thank you and good luck!

Check Out My Other Books

Below you'll find some of my other popular books that are popular on Amazon and Kindle as well. Simply click on the links below to check them out. Alternatively, you can visit my author page on Amazon to see other work done by me.

C ++ Programming Success in a Day

Android Programming in a Day

PHP Programming Professional Made Easy

C Programming Success in a Day

CSS Programming Professional Made Easy

C Programming Professional Made Easy

JavaScript Programming Made Easy

HTML Professional Programming Made Easy

the rest of Python Programming in a Day

If the links do not work, for whatever reason, you can simply search for these titles on the Amazon website to find them.